T0311074

Photographer • Joelle Blanchard
Design Layout • Quail Studio
Models • Bowen Geigley, Lotus Geigley, Zora Hayter, Daltry Hughes,
Laiya Kha, Azul Martinez, Luca Martinez, Amner Martinez, Laura Rodriguez,
Nyayop Chuol Toang, Toang Chuol Toang

All rights reserved. Reproduction in whole or any part
of all material, including illustrations, in this magazine is strictly
forbidden. No part may be reproduced, stored in a retrieval
system, or transmitted in any form or by any means electronic,
electrostatic, magnetic tape, mechanical photocopying, recording
or otherwise without prior permission of the copyright owners
having been given in writing. The designs in this magazine are
copyrighted and must not be knitted for re-sale. Reproduction
of this publication is protected by copyright and is sold on the
condition that it used for non-commercial purposes. Yarn quantities
are approximate as they are based on average requirements.
Colour reproduction is as close as printing will allow.

First published in Great Britain in 2019 by
Quail Publishing Limited
Old Town Hall, Market Square, Buckingham, Buckinghamshire, MK18 1NJ
E-mail: info@quailstudio.co.uk

ISBN: 978-0-9935908-9-4

© Quail Publishing Ltd, 2019

CONTENTS

—

JORGE

page 50

—

FRANCIS

page 52

—

LIAM

page 54

—

PERI

page 56

—

LENNON

page 58

ZOE

page 60

—

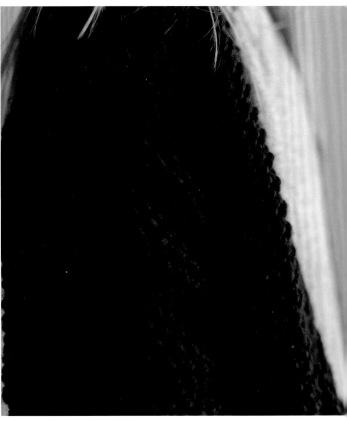

FLETCHER

page 62

—

TRIP HAT AND
DALTRY JUMPER

page 64 & 66

ESME

page 68

—

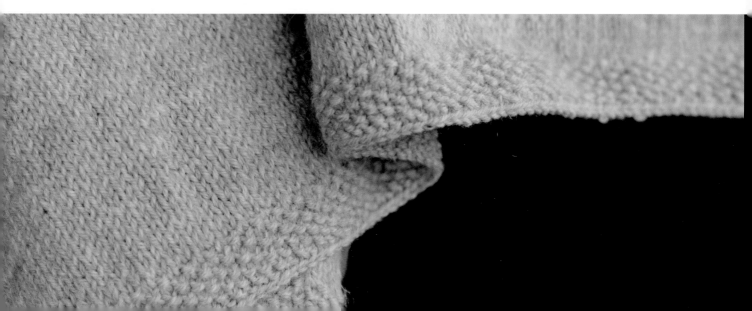

RORY

page 70

—

ROBIN

page 72

—

SCOUT

page 74

—

ZANE

page 76

—

RAMONA

GIRLS

page 78

—

RAMONA
WOMENS

page 80

—

PEPPER
SKIRT
AND
LOTUS
CARDIGAN

page 82 & 84

BOWEN

page 88

—

STORY

page 90

—

REMI

page 92

—

JORGE

SIZES

To fit age	3 - 4	5 - 6	7 - 8	9 - 10	11 - 12	years
To fit chest	61	66	71	76	81	cm
	24	26	28	30	32	in
Actual Size	67.5	74	77	83	86	cm
	26½	29¼	30¼	32¾	33¾	in

YARN

Rowan Brushed Fleece (photographed in Peat 00262)

	3	4	4	5	5	x 50g

NEEDLES

6mm (no 4) (US 10) circular needle 60 [60: 60: 60: 80] cm
(24 [24: 24: 24: 32] in) long
6mm (no 4) (US 10) circular needle no more than 40 cm (16 in) long
6mm (no 4) (US 10) set of 4 double-pointed needles (DPNs)

EXTRAS

Stitch markers
Stitch holders

TENSION

13 sts and 19 rnds to 10 cm (4 in) measured over st st
using 6mm (US 10) needles.

SPECIAL ABBREVIATIONS

M1L – insert tip of left needle from front to back
under the bar between the last st and the next st,
K into the back of it; M1R – insert tip of left needle
from back to front under the bar between the last st
and the next st, K into the back of it.

Note: Pullover is worked in one piece from top down.
Yoke is worked in rows then joined in the round after
neck shaping. Body and sleeves are worked
in rounds.

YOKE

Using longer 6mm (US 10) circular needle cast on
18 [20: 20: 22: 22] sts. Do not join, work back and
forth in rows.
Set-up row (WS): P1 (right front), PM, P2 (right sleeve),
PM, P12 [14: 14: 16: 16] (back); PM, P2 (left sleeve),
PM, P1 (left front).
Shape raglan
Row 1 (inc row) (RS): K1, M1R, Sl M, K1, M1L, K1, M1R,
Sl M; K1, M1L, K10 [12: 12: 14: 14], M1R, K1, Sl M, M1L,
K1, M1R, K1, Sl M, M1L, K1. 26 [28: 28: 30: 30] sts.

Row 2: *P to M, Sl M; rep from * 3 times more,
P to end.
Row 3 (inc row) (RS): K to 1 st before first M, M1R, K1,
Sl M, *K1, M1L, K to 1 st before next M, M1R, K1, Sl M;
rep from * twice more, K1, M1L, K to end.
Row 4: As row 2.
Continue in this way, inc 8 sts as set on next and
every foll alt row/rnd 10 [11: 12: 13: 14] times, then on
foll 4th rnd once, ending last rnd at beg of
left sleeve.
AT THE SAME TIME, shape front neck as follows:
After first 4 rows of raglan shaping have been
worked, inc 1 st at each end of next and every foll
4th row 2 [2: 3: 3: 4] times, then on every foll alt row
2 [3: 2: 3: 2] times. Do not turn after last neck inc row.
Join fronts and continue working in the rnds (every
rnd K) until all raglan incs have been completed.
140 [152: 160: 172: 180] sts (Back and front will each
have 40 [44: 46: 50: 52] sts; sleeves will each have
30 [32: 34: 36: 38] sts).
Remove markers.
Divide for body and sleeves
Next rnd: Place first 30 [32: 34: 36: 38] sts on holder
for left sleeve; cast on 4 sts for underarm and PM for
beg of rnd between 2nd and 3rd of these sts;
K40 [44: 46: 50: 52] sts for back; place next 30 [32: 34:
36: 38] sts on holder for right sleeve; cast on 4 sts for
underarm; K40 [44: 46: 50: 52] sts for front, then K to
M. 88 [96: 100: 108: 112] sts for body rem on needle
(Back and front each have 44 [48: 50: 54: 56] sts).

BODY

Slipping M at beg of every rnd, continue working in rnds of st st (every rnd K) until body meas 24 [26: 28: 29: 30.5] cm from underarm.

Next rnd: Sl M, *K1, P1: rep from * to M.

Last rnd forms rib.

Rep last rnd until rib meas 4 [4.5: 5: 5: 5] cm.

Cast off **loosely** in rib.

SLEEVES (both alike)

Starting at underarm, transfer one set of sleeve sts from st holder to 6mm (US 10) DPNs.

With RS facing, rejoin yarn and pick up and K4 cast on underarm sts and PM for beg of rnd between 2nd and 3rd of these sts, K to M. 34 [36: 38: 40: 42] sts.

Begin working in rnds of st st (every rnd K).

Next rnd: Sl M, K to M.

Rep last rnd 1 [3: 5: 9: 11] times more.

Next (dec) rnd: Sl M, K2tog, K to 2 sts before M, SSK.

Next 5 rnds: Sl M, K to M.

Rep last 6 rnds 5 [5: 6: 6: 7] times more.

22 [24: 24: 26: 26] sts.

Slipping M at beg of every rnd, continue working in rnds of st st until sleeve meas 22.5 [24.5: 28: 30.5: 34.5] cm.

Next rnd: Sl M, *K1, P1; rep from * to M.

Last rnd forms rib.

Rep last rnd until rib meas 4 [4.5: 5: 5: 5] cm.

Cast off **loosely** in rib.

Making Up

Press as described on the information page.

Neckband

With RS facing, shorter 6mm (US 10) circular needle and starting at centre front neck edge, pick up and K 12 [13: 14: 15: 16] sts up right side of front neck, 2 sts from right sleeve, 12 [14: 14: 16: 16] across back neck, 2 sts from left sleeve and 12 [13: 14: 15: 16] sts down left side of front neck. 40 [44: 46: 50: 52] sts.

Do not join, work back and forth in rows.

Row 1: *K1, P1; rep from to end.

Last row forms rib.

Rep last row 4 (5: 5: 6: 6) times more.

Cast off **loosely** in rib.

Sew side edges of neckband in position, overlapping left side over right side.

Sew underarm to close and neaten gap, if necessary.

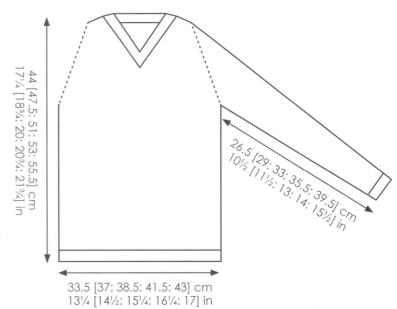

44 [47.5: 51: 53: 55.5] cm
17¼ [18¾: 20: 20¾: 21¾] in

26.5 [29: 33: 35.5: 39.5] cm
10½ [11½: 13: 14: 15½] in

33.5 [37: 38.5: 41.5: 43] cm
13¼ [14½: 15¼: 16¼: 17] in

FRANCIS
—

SIZES

To fit age	3 - 4	5 - 6	7 - 8	9 - 10	11 - 12	years
To fit chest	61	66	71	76	81	cm
	24	26	28	30	32	in
Actual Size	64.5	71	74	83	86	cm
	25½	28	29¼	32¾	33¾	in

YARN

Rowan Brushed Fleece (photographed in Rock 00273)

	5	5	6	6	7	x 50g

NEEDLES

6mm (no 4) (US 10) circular needle 60 [60: 60: 60: 80] cm
(24 [24: 24: 32: 32] in) long
6mm (no 4) (US 10) set of 4 double-pointed needles (DPNs)

EXTRAS

Stitch markers
Stitch holders

TENSION

13 sts and 19 rnds to 10 cm (4 in) measured over st st
using 6mm (US 10) needles.

SPECIAL ABBREVIATIONS

M1L – insert tip of left needle from front to back under
the bar between the last st and the next st, K into the
back of it;
M1R – insert tip of left needle from back to front
under the bar between the last st and the next st,
K into the back of it.

Note: Dress is worked in one piece from top down.
Yoke is worked in rows then joined in the round after
neck shaping. Body and sleeves are worked
in rounds.

YOKE

Using 6mm (US 10) circular needle cast on
18 [20: 20: 22: 22] sts. Do not join, work back and forth
in rows.
Set-up row (WS): P1 (right front), PM, P2 (right sleeve),
PM, P12 [14: 14: 16: 16] (back), PM, P2 (left sleeve),
PM, P1 (left front).
Shape raglan
Row 1 (inc row) (RS): K1, M1R, Sl M, K1, M1L, K1, M1R,
Sl M, K1, M1L, K10 [12: 12: 14: 14], M1R, K1, Sl M, M1L,
K1, M1R, K1, Sl M, M1L, K1. 26 [28: 28: 30: 30] sts.

Row 2: *P to M, Sl M, rep from * 3 times more,
P to end.
Row 3 (inc row) (RS): K to 1 st before first M, M1R, K1,
Sl M, *K1, M1L, K to 1 st before next M, M1R, K1, Sl M;
rep from * twice more, K1, M1L, K to end.
Row 4: As row 2.
Continue in this way inc 8 sts as set on next and every
foll alt row/rnd 8 [9: 10: 11: 12] times, then on every
4th rnd twice, ending last rnd at beg of left sleeve.
AT THE SAME TIME, shape front neck as follows:
After first 4 rows of raglan shaping have been
worked, cast on 1 [2: 2: 2: 2] sts at beg of next 2 rows,
then 2 sts at beg of following 2 rows.
Cast on 4 [4: 4: 6: 6] sts for centre front at beg of
next row.
Do not turn.
Join fronts and continue working in rnds of st st (every
rnd K) until all raglan incs have been complted.
132 [144: 152: 164: 172] sts (Back and front will each
have 38 [42: 44: 48: 50] sts; sleeves will each have
28 [30: 32: 34: 36] sts).
Remove markers.
Divide for body and sleeves
Next rnd: Place first 28 [30: 32: 34: 36] sts on holder for
left sleeve; cast on 4 [4: 4: 6: 6] sts for underarm and
PM for beg of rnd in the middle of these sts; K38 [42:
44: 48: 50] sts for back; place next 28 [30: 32: 34: 36] sts
on holder for right sleeve; cast on 4 [4: 4: 6: 6] sts for
underarm; K38 [42: 44: 48: 50] sts for front, then K to M.
84 [92: 96: 108: 112] sts for body rem on needle (Back
and front each have 42 [46: 48: 54: 56] sts).

BODY

Next rnd: Sl M, *P3, K36 [40: 42: 48: 50] sts, P3; rep from * once more.

Rep last rnd until body meas 38 [44.5: 51: 54.5: 58.5] cm from underarm.

Next rnd: Sl M, *K1, P1; rep from * to M.

Last rnd forms rib.

Rep last rnd until rib meas 5 cm.

Cast off **loosely** in rib.

SLEEVES (both alike)

Starting at underarm, transfer one set of sleeve sts from stitch holder to 6mm (US 10) DPNs.

With RS facing, rejoin yarn and pick up K4 [4: 4: 6: 6] cast on underarm sts and PM for beg of rnd in centre of these sts, K to M. 32 [34: 36: 38: 42] sts.

Beg working in rnds of st st (every rnd K).

Next rnd: Sl M, K to M.

Rep last rnd 5 [1: 7: 1: 5] times more.

Next (dec) rnd: Sl M, K2tog, K to 2 sts before M, SSK.

Next 5 [7: 7: 7: 7] rnds: Sl M, K to M.

Rep last 6 [8: 8: 8: 8] rnds 5 [5: 5: 6: 6] times more. 20 [22: 24: 26: 28] sts.

Slipping M at beg of every rnd, continue working in rnds of st st until sleeve meas 24 [28.5: 32: 33: 34.5] cm.

Next rnd: Sl M, *K1, P1; rep from * to M.

Last rnd forms rib.

Rep last rnd until rib meas 4 [4.5: 5: 5: 5] cm.

Cast off **loosely** in rib.

Making Up

Press as described on the information page.

Neckband

With RS facing, 6mm (US 10) DPNs and starting at right back raglan, pick up and K 12 [14: 14: 16: 16] sts across back neck, 2 sts from left sleeve, 16 [18: 18: 20: 20] sts evenly around front neck and 2 sts from right sleeve. 32 [36: 36: 40: 40] sts. Join and PM for beg of rnd.

Rnd 1: Sl M, *K1, P1; rep from to M.

Last rnd forms rib.

Rep last rnd 4 [5: 5: 6: 6] times more.

Cast off **loosely** in rib.

Sew underarm to close and neaten gap, if necessary.

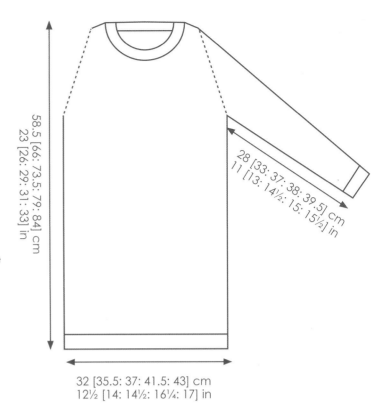

58.5 [66: 73.5: 79: 84] cm
23 [26: 29: 31: 33] in

28 [33: 37: 38: 39.5] cm
11 [13: 14½: 15: 15½] in

32 [35.5: 37: 41.5: 43] cm
12½ [14: 14½: 16¼: 17] in

LIAM

SIZE

	S	M	L	XL	XXL	
To fit chest	86.5	96.5	106.5	117	127	cm
	34	38	42	46	50	in
Actual Size	91	100	111	120	131	cm
	35¾	39¼	43¾	47¼	51½	in

YARN

Rowan Alpaca Soft DK (photographed in Charcoal 211)

	S	M	L	XL	XXL	
	9	10	10	11	12	x 50g

NEEDLES

4mm (no 8) (US 6) circular needle, 80 cm (32 in) long
4mm (no 8) (US 6) circular needle, 40 cm (16 in)long
4mm (no 8) (US 6) set of 4 double-pointed needles

EXTRAS

Stitch markers
Stitch holders

TENSION

22 sts and 30 rnds to 10 cm (4 in) measured over st st using 4mm (US 6) needles.

SPECIAL ABBREVIATIONS

M1L – insert tip of left needle from front to back under the bar between the last st and the next st, K into the back of it;
M1R – insert tip of left needle from back to front under the bar between the last st and the next st, K into the back of it

Note: Pullover is worked in one piece from top down. Yoke is worked in rows then joined in the round after neck shaping. Body and sleeves are worked in rounds.

YOKE

Using longer 4mm (US 6) circular needle cast on 48 [54: 60: 70: 76] sts. Do not join, work back and forth in rows.
Set-up row (WS): P1 (right front), PM, P6 [6: 6: 8: 8] (right sleeve), PM, P34 [40: 46: 52: 58] (back); PM, P6 [6: 6: 8: 8] (left sleeve), PM, P1 (left front).
Shape raglan
Row 1 (inc row) (RS): K1, M1R, SI M, *K1, M1L, K to 1 st before M, M1R, K1, SI M; rep from * twice more, M1L,

K1. 56 [62: 68: 78: 84] sts.
Row 2: *P to M, SL M; repeat from * 3 times more, P to end.
Row 3 (inc row) (RS): K to 1 st before first M, M1R, K1, SI M, *K1, M1L, K to 1 st before next M, M1R, K1, SI M; rep from * twice more, K1, M1L, K to end.
Row 4: As row 2.
Cont in this way inc 8 sts as set on next and every foll alt row/rnd 22 [24: 28: 30: 34] times, then on every 4th rnd 3 [3: 2: 2: 1] times, ending last rnd at beg of left sleeve.
AT THE SAME TIME shape front neck as follows:
After first 4 rows of raglan shaping have been worked, cast on 1 st at beg of next 2 rows, 2 sts at beg of foll 4 rows, then 3 sts at beg of next 2 rows. Cast on 16 [22: 28: 34: 40] sts for centre front at beg of next row. Do not turn.
Join fronts and continue working in rnds of st st (every rnd K) until all raglan incs have been completed. 304 [332: 368: 400: 436] sts (Back and front will each have 90 [100: 112: 122: 134] sts; sleeves will each have 62 [66: 72: 78: 84] sts).
Remove markers.
Divide for body and sleeves
Next rnd: Place first 62 [66: 72: 78: 84] sts on holder for left sleeve; cast on 10 sts for underarm and PM for beg of rnd between 5th and 6th of these sts; K90 [100: 112: 122: 134] sts for back; place next 62 [66: 72: 78: 84] sts on holder for right sleeve; cast on 10 sts for underarm; K90 [100: 112: 122: 134] sts for front, then K to M. 200 [220: 244: 264: 288] sts for

body rem on needle (Back and front each have
100 [110: 122: 132: 144] sts).

BODY
Slipping M at beg of every rnd, continue working in
rnds of st st (every rnd K) until body meas
44.5 [45.5: 47: 48: 48] cm from underarm.
Next rnd: Sl M, *K1, P1; rep from * to M.
This rnd forms rib.
Rep last rnd until rib meas 6.5 cm.
Cast off **loosely** in rib.

SLEEVES (both alike)
Starting at underarm, transfer one set of sleeve sts
from stitch holder to 4mm (US 6) DPNs.
With RS facing, rejoin yarn and pick up and K10 cast
on underarm sts and PM for beg of rnd between 5th
and 6th of these sts, K to M. 72 [76: 82: 88: 94] sts.
Work in rnds of st st (every rnd K).
Next rnd: Sl M, K to M.
Rep last rnd 13 [9: 11: 7: 5] times more.
Next (dec) rnd: Sl M, K2tog, K to 2 sts before M, SSK.
Next 7 rnds: Sl M, K to M.
Rep last 8 rnds 10 [11: 9: 9: 4] times more.
50 [52: 62: 68: 84] sts.
Next (dec) rnd: Sl M, K2tog, K to 2 sts before M, SSK.
Next 5 rnds: Sl M, K to M.
Rep last 6 rnds 0 [0: 3: 4: 12] times more.
48 [50: 54: 58: 58] sts.
Slipping M at beg of every rnd, continue working in
rnds of st st until sleeve meas 39.5 [40.5: 42: 43: 44.5]cm.
Next rnd: Sl M, *K1, P1; rep from * to M.
Last rnd forms rib.
Rep last rnd until rib meas 6.5 cm.
Cast off **loosely** in rib.

Making Up
Press as described on the information page.
Neckband
With RS facing, shorter 4mm (US 6)circular needle
and starting at right back raglan, pick up and
K 34 [40: 46: 52: 58] sts across back neck,
6 [6: 6: 8: 8] sts from left sleeve, 44 [50: 56: 62: 68] sts
evenly around front neck, 6 [6: 6: 8: 8] sts from
right sleeve.
90 [102: 114: 130: 142] sts.
Join and PM for beg of rnd.
Rnd 1: Sl M, *K1, P1; rep from to M.
Last round forms rib.
Rep last rnd 9 times more.
Cast off **loosely** in rib.
Sew underarm to close and neaten gap,
if necessary.

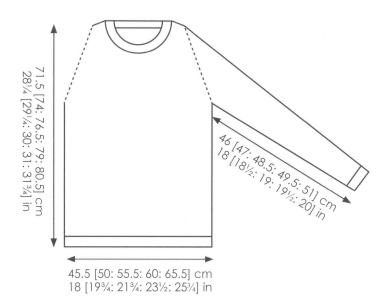

71.5 [74: 76.5: 79: 80.5] cm
28¼ [29¼: 30: 31: 31¾] in

46 [47: 48.5: 49.5: 51] cm
18 [18½: 19: 19½: 20] in

45.5 [50: 55.5: 60: 65.5] cm
18 [19¾: 21¾: 23½: 25¾] in

PERI

SIZE
One Size
78cm/30¾ in circumference x 49cm/19½ in to point

YARN
Big Wool (photographed in Glum 56)
3 x 100gm

NEEDLES
1 pair 9mm (no 00) (US 13) needles
9mm (no 00) (US 13) circular needle, 40 cm (14 in) long

EXTRAS
Stitch marker

TENSION
9 sts and 20 rows to 10 cm (4 in) measured over
garter st using 9mm (US 13) needles.

COWL
Using 9mm (US 13) needle cast on 1 st.
Row 1: Kfb. 2 sts
Row 2: Kfb, K1. 3 sts

Row 3: Kfb, K to end.
Rep last row until there are 49 sts.

Change to 9mm (US 13) circular needle.

Next row: Cast on 20 sts, Kfb, K 48. 70 sts.
Do not turn work. Place marker at end of last row
and move this marker up at end of every rnd.

Join in rnd, taking care not to twist sts.
Rnd 1: * K1, P1, rep from * to end.
This rnd forms single rib.
Repeat last rnd until single rib section meas 25 cm.
Cast off in rib.

MAKING UP
Press as described on the information page.

LENNON
—

SIZE
One Size
122cm/48in width x 20cm/8in length

YARN
Big Wool (photographed in Concrete 61)
3 x 100gm

NEEDLES
9mm (no 00) (US 13) circular needle 80 cm (32 in) long

EXTRAS
Stitch marker

TENSION
10 sts and 18 rnds to 10 cm (4 in) measured over
linen st patt using 9mm (US 13) needle

COWL
Using 9mm (US 13) needle, cast on 122 sts.
Place marker at end of cast on edge and move this
marker up at end of every rnd.

Join in rnd, taking care not to twist sts.
Rnd 1: Purl.
Rnd 2: Knit.
Rnd 3: Purl.
Rnd 4: K1, *bring yarn to front, sl 1, take yarn back,
k1, rep from * to end.
Rnd 5: Bring yarn to front, sl 1, take yarn back,
*k1, bring yarn to front, sl 1, take yarn back,
rep from * to end.

Rnds 4 - 5 form linen st patt.
Cont in linen st patt until work meas 19 cm from cast
on edge.

Now work rounds 1-2 again.
Cast off purlwise.

MAKING UP
Press as described on the information page.

ZOE
—

SIZES

To fit age	3 - 4	5 - 6	7 - 8	9 - 10	11 - 12	years
To fit chest	61	66	71	76	81	cm
	24	26	28	30	32	in
Actual Size	64	72	80	88	96	cm
	25¼	28¼	31½	34¾	37¾	in

YARN

Rowan Big Wool (photographed in Smoky 007)

5	6	7	9	9	x 100gm

NEEDLES

1 pair 8mm (no 0) (US 11) needles
1 pair 9mm (no 00) (US 13) needles
9mm (no 00) (US 13) circular needle 80 cm (32 in) long

EXTRAS
Stitch markers

TENSION
10 sts and 15 rows to 10 cm (4 in) measured over moss st using 9mm (US 13) needles.

BACK
Using 8mm (US 11) needles cast on
32 [36: 40: 44: 48] sts.
Row 1: *K1, P1; rep from * to end.
This row forms rib.
Work in rib for a further 5 rows, ending with a RS facing for next row.
Change to 9mm (US 13) needles.
Row 1 (RS): *K1, P1; rep from * to end.
Row 2: *P1, K1; rep from * to end.
These 2 rows form moss st patt.
Cont in patt until back meas 58.5 [66: 73.5: 79: 84] cm, ending with RS facing for next row.
Cast off in patt.

LEFT FRONT
Using 8mm (US 11) needles cast on
12 [14: 16: 18: 20] sts.
Work in rib as given for back for 6 rows, ending with a RS facing for next row.
Change to 9mm (US 13) needles.
Beg with row 1, now work in moss st patt as given for back until left front meas 58.5 [66: 73.5: 79: 84] cm, ending with RS facing for next row.
Cast off in patt.

RIGHT FRONT
Work as given for left front.

SLEEVES (both alike)
Using 8mm (US 11) needles cast on
14 [16: 18: 18: 20] sts.
Work in rib as given for back for 6 rows, ending with a RS facing for next row.
Change to 9mm (US 13) needles.
Beg with row 1, now work in moss st patt as given for back, shaping sides by inc 1 st at each end of
1st [3rd: 3rd: 5th: 5th] and every foll 4th row until there are 34 [36: 40: 42: 44] sts, taking inc sts into patt.
Cont straight until sleeve meas 32 [34.5: 38: 42: 43] cm, ending with RS facing for next row.
Cast off in patt.

POCKETS (make 2)
Using 8mm (US 11) needles cast on 10 [10: 12: 12: 12] sts for top edge.
Work in rib as on back for 4 rows, ending with a RS facing for next row.
Beg with row 1, now work in moss st patt as given for back until pocket meas 11.5 [11.5: 12.5: 12.5: 12.5] cm, ending with a RS facing for next row.
Cast off in patt.

MAKING UP
Press as described on the information page.
Join both shoulder seams using back stitch, or
mattress stitch if preferred.

Front/Neck border
With RS facing and using 9mm (US 13) circular
needle, pick up and K128 [144: 160: 170: 182] sts
evenly along entire front/back neck opening edge,
starting at right front cast-on edge and ending at left
front cast on edge. Do not join, work back and forth
in rows.
Beg with row 2, work in rib for 5 rows, ending with a
RS facing for next row.
Cast off **loosely** in rib.

Mark depth of armholes at side edges of fronts
and back 17 [18.5: 20: 21.5: 22] cm down from
shoulder seams.
See information page for finishing instructions,
setting in sleeves between markers using the straight
cast-off method.
Join side and sleeve seams. Using photograph as a
guide, sew pockets onto fronts.

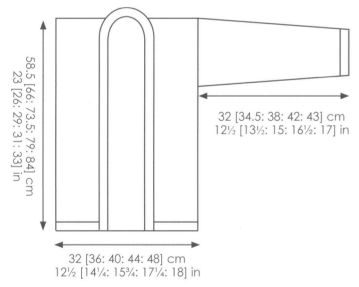

58.5 [66: 73.5: 79: 84] cm
23 [26: 29: 31: 33] in

32 [34.5: 38: 42: 43] cm
12½ [13½: 15: 16½: 17] in

32 [36: 40: 44: 48] cm
12½ [14¼: 15¾: 17¼: 18] in

FLETCHER
—

SIZE
One Size
20cm/8in width x 200cm/79in length

YARN
Rowan Alpaca Soft DK
A: Marine Blue 212
4 x 50gm
B: Rainy Day 210
4 x 50gm

NEEDLES
4mm (no 8) (US 6) circular needle 40 cm (16 in) long

EXTRA
Stitch marker

TENSION
22 sts and 30 rnds to 10 cm (4 in) measured over st st using 4mm (US 6) needle

SCARF
Using 4mm (US 6) needle and yarn A cast on 88 sts.

Place marker at end of cast on edge and move this marker up at end of every rnd.

Join in rnd, taking care not to twist sts.

Rnd 1: *K2, P2, rep from * to end.
This rnd forms 2 x 2 rib.
Cont in 2 x 2 rib until work meas 15 cm from cast on edge.

Next Rnd: Using yarn B, K to end.
Last rnd forms st st.

Cont in st st for a further 29 rnds.

Using yarn A, cont in st st for 30 rnds.

Repeat last 60 rnds until work meas approx 185 cm from cast on edge, ending with rnd 30 of stripe B.

Using yarn A, work in 2 x 2 rib for 15 cm.
Cast off in rib.

MAKING UP
Press as described on the information page.

.

TRIP
—

SIZE
One Size

YARN
Big Wool (photographed in Glum 056)
1 x 100gm

NEEDLES
10mm (no 000) (US 15) circular needle 40 cm (16 in) long
Set of four 10mm (no 000) (US 15) double pointed needles

EXTRAS
Stitch marker

TENSION
8 sts and 12 rnds to 10 cm (4 in) measured over st st
using 10mm (US 15) needles

HAT
Using 10mm (US 15) circular needle cast on 42 sts.
Place marker at end of cast on edge and move this
marker up at end of every rnd.

Join in rnd, taking care not to twist sts.

Rnd 1: *K1, P2, rep from * to end.
This rnd forms rib.
Cont in rib until work meas 25 cm.

Shape top
Change to double pointed needles when necessary.
Rnd 1: *K1, P2tog, rep from * to end. 28 sts
Rnd 2: *K1, P1, repeat from * to end.
Rnd 3: * P2tog, rep from * to end. 14 sts
Break yarn and thread through rem 14 sts.
Pull up tight and fasten off securely.

MAKING UP
Press as described on the information page.

DALTRY

—

SIZES

To fit age	3 - 4	5 - 6	7 - 8	9 - 10	11 - 12	years
To fit chest	61	66	71	76	81	cm
	24	26	28	30	32	in
Actual Size	64	71	73	80	86	cm
	25¼	28	28¾	31½	33¾	in

YARN

Rowan Big Wool (photographed in Smokey 007)

4	5	5	6	7	x 50gm

NEEDLES

9mm (no 00) (US 13) circular needle no more than 60 [60: 60: 80: 80] cm
(24 [24: 24: 32: 32] in)long
9mm (no 00) (US 13) set of 4 double-pointed needles (DPNs)

EXTRAS
Stitch markers
Stitch holders

TENSION
9 sts and 13 rnds to 10 cm (4 in) measured over st st using 9mm (US 13) needles.

SPECIAL ABBREVIATIONS
M1L – insert tip of left needle from front to back under the bar between the last st and the next st, K into the back of it;
M1R – insert tip of left needle from back to front under the bar between the last st and the next st, K into the front of it;
M1P – insert tip of left needle from front to back under one strand between the last st and the next st on cast on row, P into the back of it.

Note: Pullover is worked in one piece from top down. Yoke is worked in rows then joined in the round after neck shaping. Body and sleeves are worked in rounds.

YOKE
Using 9mm (US 13) circular needle cast on 14 [15: 16: 17: 18] sts. Do not join, work back and forth in rows.
Set-up row (WS): P1 (right front), PM, P1, M1P, P1 (right sleeve), PM, P2, M1P, P4 [5: 6: 7: 8], M1P, P2 (back); PM, P1, M1P, P1 (left sleeve), PM, P1 (left front).
18 [19: 20: 21: 22] sts.

Shape raglan
Row 1 (inc row) (RS): K1, M1R, SI M, K1, M1L, K1, M1R, K1, SI M, K1, M1L, K8 [9: 10: 11: 12], M1R, K1, SI M, K1, M1L, K1, M1R, K1, SI M, M1L, K1. 26 [27: 28: 29: 30] sts.
Row 2: * P to M, SL M, repeat from * 3 times more, P to end.
Row 3 (inc row): K to 1 st before first M, M1R, K1, SI M, *K1, M1L, K to 1 st before next M, M1R, K1, SI M; rep from * twice more, K1, M1L, K to end.
Row 4: As row 2.
Cont in this way inc 8 sts as set on next and every foll alt row/rnd 4 [5: 4: 5: 6] times, then on 4th rnd 1 [1: 2: 2: 2 times ending last rnd at beg of left sleeve.
AT THE SAME TIME shape front neck as follows:
After first 4 rows of raglan shaping have been worked, cast on 1 st at beg of next 2 rows and 1 [1: 2: 2: 2] sts at beg of foll 2 rows. Cast on 4 [5: 4: 5: 6] sts for centre front at beg of next row. Do not turn.
Join fronts and continue working in rnds of st st (every rnd K) until all raglan incs have been completed. 90 [100: 102: 112: 122] sts (Back and front will each have 26 [29: 30: 33: 36] sts; sleeves will each have 19 [21: 21: 23: 25] sts).
Remove markers.

Divide for body and sleeves
Next rnd: Place first 19 [21: 21: 23: 25] sts on holder for left sleeve; cast on 3 sts for underarm and PM for beg of rnd between 1st and 2nd of these sts; K26 [29: 30: 33: 36] sts for back; place next

19 [21: 21: 23: 25] sts on holder for right sleeve; cast on 3 sts for underarm; K26 [29: 30: 33: 36] sts for front, then K to M. 58 [64: 66: 72: 78] sts for body rem on needle (Back and front each have 29 [32: 33: 36: 39] sts).

BODY
Slipping M at beg of every rnd, continue working in rnds of st st (every rnd K) until body meas 20 [23: 26.5: 29: 30.5] cm from underarm.
Next rnd: SL M, *K1, P1; rep from * to M.
Last rnd forms rib.
Rep last rnd 4 times more.
Cast off **loosely** in rib.

SLEEVES (both alike)
Starting at underarm, transfer one set of sleeve sts from stitch holder to 9mm (US 13) DPNs.
With RS facing, rejoin yarn and pick up and K3 cast on underarm sts and PM for beg of rnd between 1st and 2nd of these sts, K to M. 22 [24: 24: 26: 28] sts.
Begin working in rounds of st st (every rnd K).
Next rnd: Sl M, K to M.
Rep last rnd 2 [6: 8: 4: 6] times more.
Next (dec) rnd: Sl M, K2tog, K to 2 sts before M, SSK.
Next 5 rnds: Sl M, K to M.
Rep last 6 rnds 3 [3: 3: 4: 4] times more.
14 [16: 16: 16: 18] sts.
Slipping M at beg of every rnd, continue working in rnds of st st until sleeve meas 23 [26.5: 30.5: 32: 34.5] cm.
Next rnd: Sl M, *K1, P1; rep from * to M.
Last rnd forms rib.
Rep last rnd 4 times more.
Cast off **loosely** in rib.

Making Up
Press as described on the information page.
Neckband
With RS facing, 9mm (US 13) DPNs and starting at right back raglan, pick up and K 8 [10: 10: 11: 12] sts across back neck, 2 sts from left sleeve,
12 [14: 14: 15: 16] sts evenly around front neck and 2 sts from right sleeve. 24 [28: 28: 30: 32] sts. Join and PM for beg of rnd.
Rnd 1: Sl M, *K1, P1; rep from to M.
Rnd 1 forms rib.
Rep rnd 1 twice more.
Cast off **loosely** in rib.
Sew underarm to close and neaten gap, if necessary.

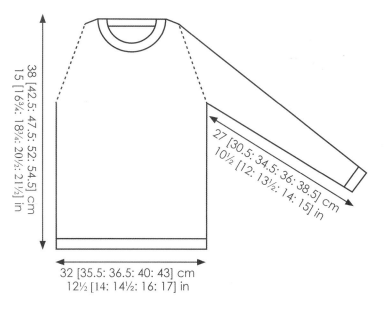

38 [42.5: 47.5: 52: 54.5] cm
15 [16¾: 18¾: 20½: 21½] in

27 [30.5: 34.5: 36: 38.5] cm
10½ [12: 13½: 14: 15] in

32 [35.5: 36.5: 40: 43] cm
12½ [14: 14½: 16: 17] in

ESME

—

SIZE
One Size
127cm/50in wide x 56cm/22in length (when folded in half)

YARN
Rowan Alpaca Soft DK (photographed in Rainy Day 210)
14 x 50gm

NEEDLES
4mm (no 8) (US 6) circular needle 60 cm (24 in) long

EXTRAS
3.5mm (US E-4) crochet hook

TENSION
22 sts and 30 rows to 10 cm (4 in) measured over st st
using 4mm (US 6) needle

PONCHO
Using 4mm (US 6) needle cast on 280 sts.
Work backwards and forwards in rows.

Row 1 (RS): *K1, P1, rep from * to end.
Row 2: *P1, K1, rep from * to end.
These 2 rows form moss st.
Work in moss st for a further 6 rows.

Next Row (RS): (K1, P1) 3 times, K to last 6 sts,
(K1, P1) 3 times.
Next Row: (P1, K1) 3 times, P to last 6 sts, (P1, K1)
3 times.
The last 2 rows set patt.
Cont in patt until work meas 56 cm from cast on
edge, ending with a WS row.

Shape neck opening
Next Row (RS): Patt 115 sts, cast off next 50 sts, patt
to end.
Next Row: Patt 115 sts, cast on 50 sts, patt to end.
280 sts.

Cont in patt until work meas 54 cm from cast on sts
for neck edge, ending with a WS row.
Row 1 (RS): *K1, P1, rep from * to end.
Row 2: *P1, K1, rep from * to end.
Work in moss st for a further 6 rows.
Cast off.

Neck edging
With RS facing and 3.5mm (US E-4) hook, slip stitch
into the first stitch on the left side of neck opening
(this counts as 1 st).
Work 1 double crochet (single crochet) into every alt
stitch around neck edge, slip stitch into first st.
Fasten off.

MAKING UP
Press as described on the information page.

Fold poncho in half. Starting at side edge 20 cm
(8 in) down from folded edge and working inwards
towards the middle, stub stitch through both layers
for 35.5 cm to denote sleeve. Work other side in
same.

RORY
—

SIZE
One Size
19cm/7½in width x 175cm/69in length

YARN
Big Wool (photographed in Prize 064)
4 x 100gm

NEEDLES
1 pair 9mm (no 00) (US 13) needles
Cable needle

TENSION
10 sts and 13 rows to 10 cm (4 in) measured over
single rib using 9mm (US 13) needles

SPECIAL ABBREVIATIONS
C6F = slip next 3 sts onto cable needle and leave at
front, K3, then K3 from cable needle
C6B = slip next 3 sts onto cable needle and leave at
back, K3, then K3 from cable needle
SSK = slip knitwise each of next 2 sts, K1, pass the 2
slipped stitches over

SCARF
Using 9mm (US 13) needles cast on 19 sts.
Row 1: K1, *P1, K1, rep from * to end.
Row 2: P1, *K1, P1, rep from * to end.

The last 2 rows form single rib.
Rep rows 1 and 2, 6 more times.

Work patt
Row 1 (WS): K3, P2tog, yrn, P11, K3.
Row 2: K3, SSK, yfwd, C6B, K8.
Row 3: K3, P2tog, yrn, P11, K3.
Row 4: K3, SSK, yfwd, K14.
Row 5: K3, P2tog, yrn, P11, K3.
Row 6: K3, SSK, yfwd, K3, C6F, K5.
Row 7: K3, P2tog, yrn, P11, K3.
Row 8: K3, SSK, yfwd, K14.
Rows 1 to 8 form patt.

Cont in patt until work meas 165 cm from cast
on edge.

Change to single rib and work for 14 rows.
Cast off in rib.

MAKING UP
Press as described on the information page.

ROBIN
—

SIZE
One Size
15.5cm/6in width x 172cm/67¾in length

YARN
Big Wool (photographed in Glum 056)
3 x 100gm

NEEDLES
1 pair 9mm (no 00) (US 13) needles

TENSION
9 sts and 13 rows to 10 cm (4 in) measured over st st
using 9mm (US 13) needles

SCARF
Using 9mm (US 13) needles cast on 14 sts.

Row 1: Sl1 kw, K1, *P1, K1, rep from * to end.
Row 1 forms single rib.
Continue in single rib until work meas 35.5 cm.

Now work in moss st
Row 1: *K1, P1, rep from * to end.
Row 2: *P1, K1, rep from * to end.
The last 2 rows form moss st.
Cont in moss stitch until work meas 50.5 cm.

Now work in garter st
Row 1: Knit.
The last row forms garter st.
Cont in garter st until work meas 157 cm.

Change to moss st and cont until work meas 172 cm.
Change to garter st and cont until work meas 208 cm.
Cast off in patt.

MAKING UP
Press as described on information page.
Fold ribbed sections in half at each end of scarf and
seam sides to make pockets.

SCOUT
—

SIZE
One Size

YARN
Rowan Cocoon (photographed in Scree 803)
2 x 100gm

NEEDLES
8mm (no 0) (US 11) circular needle 40 cm (16 in) long
Set of four 8mm (no 0) (US 11) double pointed needles

EXTRAS
Rowan Pompom (shown in Black)
Stitch marker

TENSION
14 sts and 24 rnds to 10 cm (4 in)
measured over Chinese Wave patt
using 8mm (US 11) needles

HAT
Using 8mm (US 11) needles, cast on
80 sts.
Place marker at end of cast on edge
and move this marker up at end of
every rnd.

Join in rnd, taking care not to twist sts.

Rnd 1: *K1, P1, rep from * to end.
This round forms single rib.

Repeat last rnd 8 more times.

Work patt as follows:
Rnd 1: Knit.
Rnd 2: * P1, Sl 1 with yarn in front, rep
from * to end.
Rnd 3: Knit.
Rnd 4: * Sl 1 with yarn in front, p1, rep
from * to end.

The last 4 rds form Chinese Wave patt.
Cont in patt until work meas 18 cm,
ending with rnd 4.

Shape top
Change to double pointed needles
when necessary.

Dec rnd 1: *K13, K3tog, rep from * to
end. 70 sts.
Next rnd: * P1, Sl 1 with yarn in front,
rep from * to end.

Dec rnd 2: *K11, k3tog, rep from * to
end. 60 sts.
Next rnd: * Sl 1 with yarn in front, p1,
rep from * to end.

Dec rnd 3: *K9, k3tog, rep from * to
end. 50 sts.
Next rnd: * P1, Sl 1 with yarn in front,
rep from * to end.

Dec rnd 4: *K7, k3tog, rep from * to
end. 40 sts.
Next rnd: * Sl 1 with yarn in front, p1,
rep from * to end.

Dec rnd 5: *K2tog, rep from * to end.
20 sts.

Break yarn and thread through rem
20 sts, pull up tight and fasten
off securely.

MAKING UP
Press as described on the information
page.

Attach pompom.

ZANE

—

SIZES

To fit age	3 - 4	5 - 6	7 - 8	9 - 10	11 - 12	years
To fit chest	61	66	71	76	81	cm
	24	26	28	30	32	in
Actual Size	67.5	70.5	77	83	86	cm
	26½	27¾	30¼	32¾	33¾	in

YARN

Rowan Brushed Fleece (photographed in Rock 00273)

	3	4	4	5	6	x 50gm

NEEDLES

6mm (no 4) (US 10) circular needle 60 [60: 60: 80: 80] cm
(24 [24: 24: 32: 32] in) long
6mm (no 4) (US 10) set of 4 double-pointed needles (DPNs)

EXTRAS

Stitch markers
Stitch holders

TENSION

13 sts and 19 rnds to 10 cm (4 in) measured over st st
using 6mm (US 10) needles.

SPECIAL ABBREVIATIONS

M1L – insert tip of left needle from front to back
under the bar between the last st and the next st,
K into the back of it;
M1R – insert tip of left needle from back to front
under the bar between the last st and the next st, K
into the back of it.

Note: Pullover is worked in one piece from top down.
Yoke is worked in rows then joined in the round after
neck shaping. Body and sleeves are worked
in rounds.

YOKE

Using 6mm (US 10) circular needle cast on
18 [20: 20: 22: 22] sts. Do not join, work back and
forth in rows.
Set-up row (WS): P1 (right front), PM, P2 (right sleeve),
PM, P12 [14: 14: 16: 16] (back); PM, P2 (left sleeve),
PM, P1 (leftfront).

Shape raglan

Row 1 (inc row) (RS): K1, M1R, Sl M, K1, M1L, K1, M1R,
Sl M, K1, M1L, K10 [12: 12: 14: 14], M1R, K1, Sl M, M1L,
K1, M1R, K1, Sl M, M1L, K1. 26 [28: 28: 30: 30] sts.

Row 2: * P to M, Sl M, repeat from * 3 times more,
P to end.
Row 3 (inc row) (RS): K to 1 st before first M, M1R, K1,
Sl M, *K1, M1L, K to 1 st before next M, M1R, K1, Sl M;
rep from * twice more, K1, M1L, K to end.
Row 4: As row 2.
Continue in this way inc 8 sts as set on next and
every foll alt row/rnd 11 (10: 13: 12: 13] times, then
every 4th rnd 0 [1: 0: 1: 1] time, ending last rnd at
beg of left sleeve.

AT THE SAME TIME, shape front neck as follows:
After first 4 rows of raglan shaping have been
worked, cast on 1 st at beg of next 2 rows and
1 [2: 2: 2: 2] sts at beg of foll 2 rows. Cast on
6 [6: 6: 8: 8] sts for centre front at beg of next row.
Do not turn.
Join fronts and continue working in the rnds of st st
(every rnd K) until all raglan incs have been
completed. 140 [144: 160: 164: 172] sts (Back and
front will each have 40 [42: 46: 48: 50] sts; sleeves will
each have 30 [30: 34: 34: 36] sts).
Remove markers.

Divide for body and sleeves
Next rnd: Place first 30 [30: 34: 34: 36] sts on holder for
left sleeve; cast on 4 [4: 4: 6: 6] sts for underarm and
PM for beg of rnd in middle of these sts;
K40 [42: 46: 48: 50] sts for back; place next
30 [30: 34: 34: 36] sts on holder for right sleeve; cast
on 4 [4: 4: 6: 6] sts for underarm; K40 [42: 46: 48: 50] sts for
front, then K to M. 88 [92: 100: 108: 112] sts for body
rem on needle (Back and front each have
44 [46: 50: 54: 56] sts).

BODY

Slipping M at beg of every rnd, continue working in rnds of st st (every round K) until body meas 24 [26: 28: 29: 30.5] cm from underarm.

Next rnd: Sl M, *K1, P1: rep from * to M.

Last rnd forms rib.

Rep last rnd until rib meas 4 [4.5: 5: 5: 5] cm.

Cast off **loosely** in rib.

SLEEVES (both alike)

Starting at underarm, transfer one set of sleeve stitches from stitch holder to 6mm (US 10) DPNs.

With RS facing, rejoin yarn and pick up and K4 [4: 4: 6: 6] cast on underarm sts and PM for beg of rnd in the middle of these sts, K to M.

34 [34: 38: 40: 42] sts.

Begin working in rnds of st st (every rnd K).

Next rnd: Sl M, K to M.

Rep last rnd 1 [5: 5: 5: 11] times more.

Next (dec) rnd: Sl M, K2tog, K to 2 sts before M, SSK.

Next 5 rnds: Sl M, K to M.

Rep last 6 rnds 5 [5: 6: 7: 7] times more.

22 [22: 24: 24: 26] sts.

Slipping M at beg of every rnd, continue working in rnds of st st until sleeve meas 22.5 [24.5: 28: 30.5: 34.5] cm.

Next rnd: Sl M, *K1, P1; rep from * to M.

Last rnd forms rib.

Rep last rnd until rib meas 4 [4.5: 5: 5: 5] cm.

Cast off **loosely** in rib.

Making Up

Press as described on the information page.

Neckband

With RS facing, 6mm (US 10) DPNs and starting at right back raglan, pick up and K 12 [14: 14: 16: 16] across back neck, 2 sts from left sleeve 14 [18: 18: 20: 20] sts evenly around front neck, 2 sts from right sleeve. 30 [36: 36: 40: 40] sts.

Join and PM for beg of rnd.

Rnd 1: Sl M, *K1, P1; rep from to M.

Last rnd forms rib.

Rep last rnd 4 [5: 5: 6: 6] times more.

Cast off **loosely** in rib.

Sew underarm to close and neaten gap, if necessary.

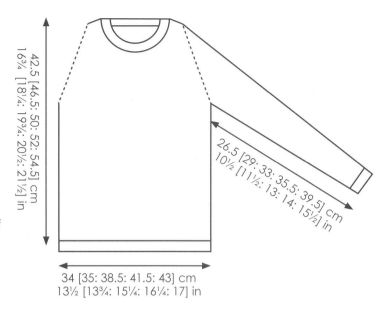

42.5 [46.5: 50: 52: 54.5] cm
16¾ [18¼: 19¾: 20½: 21½] in

26.5 [29: 33: 35.5: 39.5] cm
10½ [11½: 13: 14: 15½] in

34 [35: 38.5: 41.5: 43] cm
13½ [13¾: 15¼: 16¼: 17] in

RAMONA *GIRLS*

—

SIZE
One Size
48.5cm/19in circumference x 21cm/8¼in

YARN
Big Wool (photographed in Normandy 086)
2 x 100gm

NEEDLES
9mm (no 00) (US 13) circular needle 40 cm (16 in) long

EXTRAS
Stitch marker

TENSION
14 sts and 18 rnds to 10 cm (4 in) measured over
bramble st patt using 9mm (US 13) needle

COWL
Using 9mm (US 13) needles, cast on 68 sts.
Place marker at end of cast on edge and move this
marker up at end of every rnd.

Join in rnd, taking care not to twist sts.
Rnd 1: Purl.
Rnd 2: Knit.
Rnd 3: Purl.
Rnd 4: *(K1, P1, K1) into same st, P3tog, rep from
* to end.
Rnd 5: Knit.
Rnd 6: *P3tog, (K1, P1, K1) into same st; rep from
* to end.
Rnd 7: Knit.

Rnds 4 - 7 form bramble st patt.
Cont in bramble st patt until work meas 20 cm from
cast on edge.

Now work rnds 1-2 again.
Cast off purlwise.

MAKING UP
Press as described on the information page.

RAMONA WOMENS

—

SIZE
One Size
63cm/25in circumference x 26.5cm/10½in

YARN
Big Wool (photographed in Smoky 007)
3 x 100gm

NEEDLES
9mm (no 00) (US 13) circular needle 40 cm (16 in) long

EXTRAS
Stitch marker

TENSION
14 sts and 18 rnds to 10 cm (4 in) measured over
bramble st patt using 9mm (US 13) needle

COWL
Using 9mm (US 13) needle, cast on 88 sts.
Place marker at end of cast on edge and move this
marker up at end of every rnd.

Join in rnd, taking care not to twist sts.
Rnd 1: Purl.
Rnd 2: Knit.
Rnd 3: Purl.
Rnd 4: *(K1, P1, K1) into same st, P3tog, rep from
* to end.
Rnd 5: Knit.
Rnd 6: *P3tog, (K1, P1, K1) into same st, rep from
* to end.
Rnd 7: Knit.
Rnds 4 - 7 form bramble st patt.
Cont in bramble st patt until work meas 25.5 cm
from cast on edge.

Now work rnds 1-2 again.
Cast off purlwise.

MAKING UP
Press as described on the information page.

PEPPER

—

SIZES

To fit age	3 - 4	5 - 6	7 - 8	9 - 10	11 - 12	years
To fit waist	53	56	58.5	61	64.5	cm
	20¾	22	23	24	25½	in
Actual hip	71.5	74	79.5	82	85.5	cm
measurements	28	29¼	31¼	32¼	33¾	in

YARN

Rowan Alpaca Classic (photographed in Charcoal Mélange 102)

	3	3	4	4	5	x 25gm

NEEDLES

1 pair 3¾mm (no 9) (US 5) needles

EXTRAS – Two 19mm/¾in buttons

TENSION

23 sts and 31 rows to 10 cm (4 in) measured over st st using 3¾mm (US 5) needles.

SPECIAL ABBREVIATIONS

M1L – insert tip of left needle from front to back under the bar between the last st and the next st, K into the back of it;

M1R – insert tip of left needle from back to front under the bar between the last st and the next st, K into the front of it.

SKIRT

Using 3¾mm (US 5) needles cast on
156 [166: 176: 184: 194] sts for waist band.
Row 1 (RS): *K1, P1, rep from * to end.
Row 2: *P1, K1, rep from * to end.
These 2 rows form moss st.
Work in single rib for a further 4 rows.
Row 7 (buttonhole) (RS): Moss st 123 [129: 135: 141: 149], cast off 4 sts, moss st to last 9 sts, cast off 4 sts, moss st to end.
Row 8: Moss st 5, cast on 4 sts, moss st 20 [24: 28: 30: 32], cast on 4 sts, moss st to end.
Moss st a further 4 rows.

Work in patt as follows:
Row 1 (RS): (K1, P1) 3 times, K to last 6 sts, (K1, P1) 3 times.
Row 2: (P1, K1) 3 times, P to last 6 sts, (P1, K1) 3 times.
These two rows set patt.

Cont in patt until skirt meas 7.5 [9: 9.5: 10: 10.5] cm from cast-on edge, ending with RS facing for next row.

Hip shaping

Next row (inc) (RS): *Patt 20 [21: 19: 20: 21], M1L, K1, M1R; rep from * 6 [6: 7: 7: 7] times more, patt to end.
Next row: Patt to end.
Rep last 2 rows twice more.
198 [208: 224: 232: 240] sts.
Cont in patt until skirt meas 25.5 [29: 33: 35.5: 38] cm from cast-on edge, ending with RS facing for next row.
Now work in moss st across all sts for 9 rows, ending with WS facing for next row.
Cast off in mst.

MAKING UP

Press as described on the information page.
Try skirt on child with waistband overlapped and mark position for 2 buttons on inner layer.
Sew on buttons.

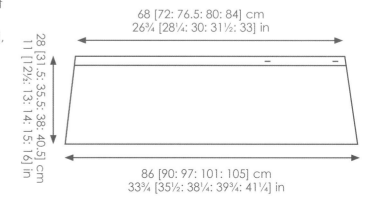

68 [72: 76.5: 80: 84] cm
26¾ [28¼: 30: 31½: 33] in

28 [31.5: 35.5: 38: 40.5] cm
11 [12½: 13: 14: 15: 16] in

86 [90: 97: 101: 105] cm
33¾ [35½: 38¼: 39¾: 41¼] in

LOTUS

SIZES

To fit age	3 - 4	5 - 6	7 - 8	9 - 10	11 - 12	years
To fit chest	61	66	71	76	81	cm
	24	26	28	30	32	in
Actual Size	66	71	76	81	87	cm
	26	28	30	32	33¾	in

YARN

Rowan Alpaca Classic (photographed in Noir 103)

	5	6	6	7	8	x 25gm

NEEDLES

1 pair 3½mm (no -) (US 4) needles
1 pair 3¾mm (no 9) (US 5) needles

EXTRAS
Stitch holders

BUTONS
5 [6: 6: 7: 7] 12mm/½in buttons

TENSION
24 sts and 31 rows to 10 cm (4 in) measured over st st using 6mm (US 10) needles.

SPECIAL ABBREVIATIONS
SSK (slip, slip, knit): slip next 2 sts knitwise, one at a time, to right needle, insert tip of left needle into fronts of these 2 sts, from left to right and K them tog;
SSP (slip, slip, purl): slip next 2 sts knitwise, one at a time, to right needle, then keeping them twisted place these 2 sts back on left needle and P them tog through back loops;
P2SP: P2tog, slip next st knitwise, return both sts to left needle, pass second st over first and slip rem st to right needle.

BACK
Using 3½mm (US 4) needles cast on 79 (85: 91: 97: 103] sts.
Row 1: *K1, P1; rep from * to last st, k1.
This row forms moss st.
Work in moss st for a further 15 rows, ending with a RS facing for next row.
Change to 3¾mm (US 5) needles.
Now work in patt as folls:
Row 1 (RS): K28 [31: 34: 37: 40], P1, YO, K1, SSK, K1, YO, K2, SSK, K5, K2tog, K2, YO, K1, K2tog, K1, YO, P1, K28 [31: 34: 37: 40].
Row 2: P28 [31: 34: 37: 40], K1, P1, YO, P1, P2tog, P1, YO, P2, P2tog, P3, SSP, P2, YO, P1, SSP, P1, YO, P1, K1, P28 [31: 34: 37: 40].
Row 3: K28 [31: 34: 37: 40], P1, K2, YO, K1, SSK, K1, YO, K2, SSK, K1, K2tog, K2, YO, K1, K2tog, K1, YO, K2, P1, K28 [31: 34: 37: 40].
Row 4: P28 [31: 34: 37: 40], K1, P3, YO, P1, P2tog, P1, YO, P2, P2SP, P2, YO, P1, SSP, P1, YO, P3, K1, P28 [31: 34: 37: 40].
Row 5: K28 [31: 34: 37: 40], P1, K4, YO, K1, SSK, K1, YO, K2, SSK, K2, K2tog, K1, YO, K4, P1, K28 [31: 34: 37: 40].
Row 6: P28 [31: 34: 37: 40], K1, P5, YO, P1, P2tog, SSP, P2, YO, P1, SSP, P1, YO, P5, K1, P28 [31: 34: 37: 40].
Row 7: K28 [31: 34: 37: 40], P1, K6, YO, K1, SSK, K1, YO, K2, SSK, K7, P1, K28 [31: 34: 37: 40].
Row 8: P28 [31: 34: 37: 40], K1, P6, SSP, P2, YO, P1, SSP, P1, YO, P7, K1, P28 [31: 34: 37: 40].
Row 9: K28 [31: 34: 37: 40], P1, K8, YO, K1, SSK, K1, YO, K2, SSK, K5, P1, K28 [31: 34: 37: 40].
Row 10: P28 [31: 34: 37: 40], K1, P4, SSP, P2, YO, P1, SSP, P1, YO, P9, K1, P28 [31: 34: 37: 40].
Row 11: K28 [31: 34: 37: 40], P1, YO, K1, SSK, K1, YO, K2, SSK, K5, K2tog, K2, YO, K1, K2tog, K1, YO, P1, K28 [31: 34: 37: 40].
Row 12: P28 [31: 34: 37: 40], SM, K1, P1, YO, P1, P2tog, P1, YO, P2, P2tog, P3, SSP, P2, YO, P1, SSP, P1, YO, P1, K1, SM, P28 [31: 34: 37: 40].
Row 13: K28 [31: 34: 37: 40], P1, K2, YO, K1, SSK, K1, YO, K2, SSK, K1, K2tog, K2, YO, K1, K2tog, K1, YO, K2, P1, K28 [31: 34: 37: 40].

Row 14: P28 [31: 34: 37: 40], K1, P3, YO, P1, P2tog, P1, YO, P2, P3tog, P2, YO, P1, SSP, P1, YO, P3, K1, P28 [31: 34: 37: 40].

Row 15: K28 [31: 34: 37: 40], P1, K4, YO, K1, SSK, K2, K2tog, K2, YO, K1, K2tog, K1, YO, K4, P1, K28 [31: 34: 37: 40].

Row 16: P28 [31: 34: 37: 40], K1, P5, YO, P1, P2tog, P1, YO, P2, P2tog, SSP, P1, YO, P5, K1, P28 [31: 34: 37: 40].

Row 17: K28 [31: 34: 37: 40], P1, K7, K2tog, K2, YO, K1, K2tog, K1, YO, K6, P1, K28 [31: 34: 37: 40].

Row 18: P28 [31: 34: 37: 40], K1, P7, YO, P1, P2tog, P1, YO, P2, P2tog, P6, K1, P28 [31: 34: 37: 40].

Row 19: K28 [31: 34: 37: 40], P1, K5, K2tog, K2, YO, K1, K2tog, K1, YO, K8, P1, K28 [31: 34: 37: 40].

Row 20: P28 [31: 34: 37: 40], K1, P9, YO, P1, P2tog, P1, YO, P2, P2tog, P4, K1 P28 [31: 34: 37: 40].
These 20 rows form lotus leaf panel patt.
Rep last 20 rows 5 [5: 6: 6: 7] times more, then first 10 rows 0 [1: 0: 1: 0] time, ending with RS facing for next row.
Cast off.

LEFT FRONT
Using 3½mm (US 4) needles cast on 39 [42: 45: 48: 51] sts.
Row 1 (RS): *K1, P1; rep from * to last 1 [0: 1: 0: 1] st, K1 [0: 1: 0: 1].
Row 2: K1 [0: 1: 0: 1], *P1, K1; rep from * to end of row.
These 2 rows form moss st.
Work a further 14 rows in moss st, ending with RS facing for next row.
Change to 3¾mm (US 5) needles.
Starting with a K row, cont in st st until left front meas 38.5 [42: 45: 48: 52.5] cm, ending with WS facing for next row.
Shape neck
Next row (WS): Cast off 8 [10: 10: 11: 11] sts, P to end. 31 [32: 35: 37: 40] sts.
Next row: K.
Next row: Cast off 3 sts, P to end. 28 [29: 32: 34: 37] sts.
Next row: K.
Next row: Cast off 2 sts, P to end. 26 [27: 30: 32: 35] sts.
Dec 1 st at neck edge on every RS row 3 times. 23 [24: 27: 29: 32] sts.
Cont straight until left front meas same as back, ending with RS facing for next row.
Cast off.

RIGHT FRONT
Using 3½mm (US 4) needles cast on 39 [42: 45: 48: 51] sts.
Row 1 (RS): P1 [0: 1: 0: 1], *K1, P1; rep from * to end.
Row 2: *P1, K1; rep from * to last 1 [0: 1: 0: 1] st, P1 [0: 1: 0: 1].
These 2 rows form moss st.
Work a further 14 rows in moss st, ending with RS facing for next row.
Change to 3¾mm (US 5) needles.
Starting with a K row, cont in st st until right front

meas 38.5 [42: 45: 48: 52.5] cm, ending with RS facing for next row.
Shape neck
Next row (RS): Cast off 8 [10: 10: 11: 11] sts, K to end. 31 [32: 35: 37: 40] sts.
Next row: P.
Next row: Cast off 3 sts, K to end. 28 [29: 32: 34: 37] sts.
Next row: P.
Next row: Cast off 2 sts, K to end. 26 [27: 30: 32: 35] sts.
Dec 1 st at neck edge on every RS row 3 times. 23 [24: 27: 29: 32] sts.
Cont straight until right front meas same as back, ending with RS facing for next row.
Cast off.

SLEEVES (both alike)
Using 3½mm (US 4) needles cast on 39 [41: 41: 45: 45] sts.
Row 1: *K1, P1; rep from * to last st, K1.
This row forms moss st.
Work in moss st for a further 15 rows, ending with a RS facing for next row.
Change to 3¾mm (US 5) needles.
Starting with a K row, cont in st st, shaping sides by inc 1 st at each end of 5th and every foll 4th row until there are 73 [79: 85: 91: 97] sts.
Cont straight until sleeve meas 32 [34.5: 38: 42: 43] cm, ending with RS facing for next row.
Cast off.

MAKING UP
Press as described on the information page.
Join both shoulder seams using back stitch, or mattress stitch if preferred.
Neckband
With RS facing and 3¾mm (US 5) needles, pick up and K 19 [22: 22: 23: 23] sts evenly along right neck edge to shoulder, 33 [37: 37: 39: 39] sts from back neck edge, 19 [22: 22: 23: 23] sts evenly along left front neck edge. 71 [81: 81: 85: 85] sts.
Row 1: *K1, P1; rep from * to last st, K1.
This row forms moss st.
Work in moss st for a further 9 rows, ending with WS facing for next row.
Cast off **loosely** in patt.
Left Front Band
With RS facing and 3¾mm (US 5) needles, pick up and K103 [125: 135: 149: 157] sts evenly along left front edge from top of neckband to cast-on edge.
Work 10 rows in moss st as given for neckband, ending with WS facing for next row.
Cast off **loosely** in patt.
Right Front Band
With RS facing and 3¾mm (US 5) needles, pick up and K103 [125: 135: 149: 157] sts evenly along right front edge from cast-on edge to top of neckband.
Work 4 rows in moss st as given for neckband, ending with WS facing for next row.

Next row (buttonhole) (WS): Moss st 4, * work 2tog, YO, moss st 21 [21: 23: 21: 22]; rep from
* 3 [4: 4: 5: 5] times more, K2tog, YO, moss st to end.
Work in moss st for a further 5 rows, ending with WS facing for next row.
Cast off **loosely** in patt.

Mark depth of armholes at side edges of fronts and back 15 [16.5: 18: 19: 20] cm down from shoulder seams. See information page for finishing instructions, setting in sleeves between markers using the straight cast-off method. Join side and sleeve seams.
Sew on buttons.

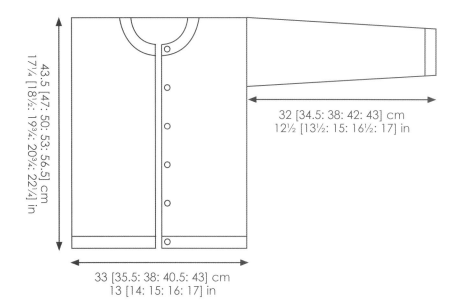

43.5 [47: 50: 53: 56.5] cm
17¼ [18½: 19¾: 20¾: 22¼] in

32 [34.5: 38: 42: 43] cm
12½ [13½: 15: 16½: 17] in

33 [35.5: 38: 40.5: 43] cm
13 [14: 15: 16: 17] in

BOWEN

SIZES

To fit age	3-4	5-6	7-8	9-10	11-12	years
To fit chest	61	66	71	76	81	cm
	24	26	28	30	32	in
Actual Size	70	74	80	85	89	cm
	27½	29	31½	33½	35	in

YARN

Rowan Alpaca Soft DK (photographed in Smoky 007)

	3-4	5-6	7-8	9-10	11-12	
A: Rainy Day 210	3	3	4	4	5	x 50gm
B: Marine Blue 212	2	2	2	2	3	x 50gm
C: Green Teal 213	1	1	1	1	1	x 50gm

NEEDLES

1 pair 4mm (no 8) (US 6) needles
3¾mm (no 9) (US 5) circular needle 80 cm (32 in) long

EXTRAS

Stitch markers
Stitch holder

BUTTONS

5 x 12mm/3/4in buttons

TENSION

22 sts and 30 rows to 10 cm (4 in) measured over st st using 4mm (US 6) needles.

BACK

Using 4mm (US 6) needles and B cast on
78 [82: 90: 94: 98] sts.
Row 1 (RS): K2, *P2, K2; rep from * to end.
Row 2: P2, *K2, P2; rep from * to end.
These 2 rows form rib.
Work in rib for a further 11 rows, ending with a WS facing for next row.
Next row: Work in rib, decreasing 0 [0: 2: 0: 0] sts evenly across. 78 [82: 88: 94: 98] sts.
Break B and join A.
Starting with a K row, cont in st st until back meas 35.5 [40.5: 44.5: 47: 49.5] cm, ending with RS facing for next row.

Shape shoulders

Cast off 13 [14: 15: 16: 16] sts at beg of next 2 rows, then 14 [14: 15: 16: 17] sts at beg of foll 2 rows.
24 [26: 28: 30: 32] sts.
Leave rem 24 [26: 28: 30: 32] sts on a holder.

LEFT FRONT

Using 4mm (US 6) needles and B cast on
40 [42: 44: 48: 50] sts.
Row 1 (RS): *K2, P2; rep from * to last 0 [2: 0: 0: 2] sts, K 0 [2: 0: 0: 2].
Row 2: P0 [2: 0: 0: 2], *K2, P2; rep from * to end.
These 2 rows form rib.
Work in rib for a further 11 rows, ending with WS facing for next row.
Next row: Work in rib, decreasing 1 [1: 0: 1: 1] st at centre. 39 [41: 44: 47: 49] sts.
Break B and join A.
Starting with a K row, cont in st st until left front meas 25.5 [30: 33: 34.5: 35.5] cm, ending with RS facing for next row. Mark beginning of last row.

Shape front neck

Next row (RS): K to last 4 sts, K2tog, K2.
Next row: P.
Rep last 2 rows 9 [10: 11: 11: 11] times more.
29 [30: 32: 35: 37] sts.
Next row (RS): K to last 4 sts, K2tog, K2.
Work 3 rows.
Rep last 4 rows 0 [0, 0, 1, 2] times more.
28 [29: 31: 33: 34] sts.
Next row (RS): K to last 4 sts, K2tog, K2.
27 [28: 30: 32: 33] sts.
Cont straight until left front matches back to beg of shoulder shaping, ending with RS facing for next row.

Shape shoulder

Cast off 13 [14: 15: 16: 16] sts at beg of next row.

Work 1 row.
Cast off rem 14 [14: 15: 16: 17] sts.

RIGHT FRONT
Using 4mm (US 6) needles and B cast on
40 [42: 44: 48: 50] sts.
Row 1 (RS): K0 [2: 0: 0: 2], *P2, K2; rep from * to end.
Row 2: *P2, K2; rep from * to last 0 [2: 0: 0: 2] sts,
P0 [2: 0: 0: 2].
These 2 rows form rib.
Work in rib for a further 11 rows, ending with WS
facing for next row.
Next row: Work in rib, decreasing 1 [1: 0: 1: 1] st at
centre. 39 [41: 44: 47: 49] sts.
Break B and join A.
Starting with a K row, cont in st st until right front
meas 25.5 [30: 33: 34.5: 35.5] cm, ending with RS
facing for next row. Mark end of last row.

Shape front neck
Next row (RS): K2, Sl1, K1, psso, K to end.
Next row: P.
Rep last 2 rows 9 [10: 11: 11: 11] times more.
29 [30: 32: 35: 37] sts.
Next row (RS): K2, Sl1, K1, psso, K to end.
Work 3 rows.
Rep last 4 rows 0 [0, 0, 1, 2] times more.
28 [29: 31: 33: 34] sts.
Next row (RS): K2, Sl1, K1, psso, K to end.
27 [28: 30: 32: 33] sts.
Cont straight until right front matches back to beg of
shoulder shaping, ending with WS facing for
next row.

Shape shoulder
Cast off 13 [14: 15: 16: 16] sts at beg of next row.
Work 1 row.
Cast off rem 14 [14: 15: 16: 17] sts.

RIGHT SLEEVE
Using 4mm (US 6) needles and B cast on
38 [38: 42: 42: 46] sts.
Row 1 (RS): K2, *P2, K2; rep from * to end.
Row 2: P2, *K2, P2; rep from * to end.
These 2 rows form rib.
Work in rib for a further 12 rows, ending with RS facing
for next row.
Break B and join A.
Starting with a K row, cont in st st, shaping sides by
inc 1 st at each end of 5th and 9 [11: 10: 13: 16] foll
4th rows, then on every foll 6th row until there are
66 [70: 76: 82: 88] sts.
Cont straight until sleeve meas 32 [34.5: 38: 42: 43] cm,
ending with RS facing for next row.
Cast off.

LEFT SLEEVE
Work as for right sleeve AND AT SAME TIME, when
sleeve meas 24 [26.5: 30: 36: 37] cm, work 6 rows with
C and then cont to end with A.

MAKING UP
Press as described on the information page.
Join both shoulder seams using back stitch, or
mattress stitch if preferred.
Front/Neck border
With RS facing, using 3¾mm (US 5) circular needle
and B, pick up and K51 [59: 65: 69: 71] sts evenly
along right front edge to marker, 28 [29: 30: 33: 36] sts
up right front neck, K24 [26: 28: 30: 32] sts from back
holder, pick up and K28 [29: 30: 33: 36] sts down left
front neck to marker, 51 [59: 65: 69: 71] sts down left
front edge. 182 [202: 218: 234: 246] sts.
Do not join, work back and forth in rows.
Beg with row 2, work in rib for 3 rows as for back,
ending with RS facing for next row.
Next row (buttonhole) (RS): Rib 4, *work 2 tog, YO, rib
9 [11: 12: 13: 14]; rep from * 3 times more, work 2 tog,
YO, rib to end.
Work a further 4 rows in rib, ending with WS facing for
next row.
Cast off **loosely** in rib.

Mark depth of armholes at side edges of fronts and
back 15 [16: 17: 18.5: 20] cm down from shoulder
seams. See information page for finishing instructions,
sewing in sleeves between markers using the straight
cast-off method. Join side and sleeve seams.
Sew on buttons.

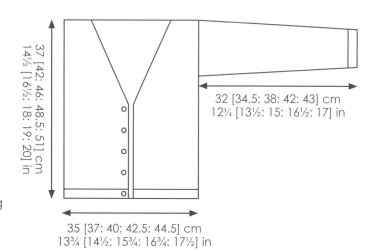

37 [42: 46: 48.5: 51] cm
14½ [16½: 18: 19: 20] in

32 [34.5: 38: 42: 43] cm
12¾ [13½: 15: 16½: 17] in

35 [37: 40: 42.5: 44.5] cm
13¾ [14½: 15¾: 16¾: 17½] in

STORY

SIZE
One Size
81cm/32in circumference x 31cm/12¼in length

YARN
Big Wool (photographed in Smoky 007)
2 x 100gm

NEEDLES
10mm (no 0) (US 15) circular needles 40 cm (16 in) long

EXTRAS
Stitch marker

TENSION
8 sts and 12 rnds to 10 cm (4 in) measured over st st
using 10mm (US 15) needle

Provisional Cast On Method
With working yarn and a length of scrap yarn
together and make a slip knot and place it on your
right hand needle (the slip knot does not count as a
st). Holding your working yarn over index finger and
the scrap yarn over thumb of left hand, cast on as
for long-tail method the number of stitches specified
in the pattern. As you cast on, you will see that your
scrap yarn creates a chain along bottom edge.
Continue with working yarn only, dropping slip knot
at end of first round.

COWL
Using 10mm (US 15) needles and provisional cast on
method, cast on 50 sts.
Place marker at end of cast on edge and move this
marker up at end of every rnd.

Join in rnd, taking care not to twist sts.
Next rnd: K to end.
The last rnd forms st st.
Cont in st st until work measures 81 cm from cast on
edge.

Grafting: Untie the slip knot from provisional cast on
edge then slowly unravel your scrap yarn stitches,
one at a time, placing live stitches onto
spare needle.
Graft or kitchener stitch ends together for
seamless join.

MAKING UP
Press as described on the information page.

REMI

SIZE
One Size
20cm/8in width x 202cm/79½in length

YARN
Big Wool (photographed in Concrete 061)
4 x 100gm

NEEDLES
1 pair 9mm (no 00) (US 13) needles

TENSION
10 sts and 13 rows to 10 cm (4 in) measured over single rib using 9mm (US 13) needles

SCARF
Using 9mm (US 13) needles cast on 20 sts.
Row 1: *K1, P1, rep from * to end.
This row forms single rib.
Rep last row 17 times more.

Now work in patt as follows
Row 1 (RS): K5, P1, yo, K2tog tbl, P1, K2, P1, yo, K2tog tbl, P1, K5.
Row 2: K3, P2, *K1, P2, rep from * to last 3 sts, K3.
Row 3: K5, P1, K2tog, yrn, P1, K2, P1, K2tog, yrn, P1, K5.
Row 4: K3, P2, *K1, P2, rep * to last 3 sts, K3.
The last 4 rows form patt.

Continue in patt until work meas 188 cm from cast on edge.

Change to single rib and work for 18 rows.
Cast off in rib.

MAKING UP
Press as described on the information page.

INFORMATION

—

TENSION

Obtaining the correct tension is perhaps the single factor which can make the difference between a successful garment and a disastrous one. It controls both the shape and size of an article, so any variation, however slight, can distort the finished garment. Different designers feature in our books and it is their tension, given at the start of each pattern, which you must match. We recommend that you knit a square in pattern and/or stocking stitch (depending on the pattern instructions) of perhaps 5 - 10 more stitches and 5 - 10 more rows than those given in the tension note. Mark out the central 10cm square with pins. If you have too many stitches to 10cm try again using thicker needles, if you have too few stitches to 10cm try again using finer needles. Once you have achieved the correct tension your garment will be knitted to the measurements indicated in the size diagram shown at the end of the pattern.

After working for hours knitting a garment, it seems a great pity that many garments are spoiled because such little care is taken in the pressing and finishing process. Follow the text below for a truly professional-looking garment.

Block out each piece of knitting and following the instructions on the ball band press the garment pieces, omitting the ribs. Tip: Take special care to press the edges, as this will make sewing up both easier and neater. If the ball band indicates that the fabric is not to be pressed, then covering the blocked out fabric with a damp white cotton cloth and leaving it to stand will have the desired effect. Darn in all ends neatly along the selvage edge or a colour join, as appropriate.

STITCHING

When stitching the pieces together, remember to match areas of colour and texture very carefully where they meet. Use a seam stitch such as back stitch or mattress stitch for all main knitting seams and join all ribs and neckband with mattress stitch, unless otherwise stated.

CONSTRUCTION

Having completed the pattern instructions, join left shoulder and neckband seams as detailed above. Sew the top of the sleeve to the body of the garment using the method detailed in the pattern, referring to the appropriate guide:
Straight cast-off sleeves: Place centre of cast-off edge of sleeve to shoulder seam.

Sew top of sleeve to body, using markers as guidelines where applicable.

Square set-in sleeves: Place centre of cast-off edge of sleeve to shoulder seam. Set sleeve head into armhole, the straight sides at top of sleeve to form a neat right-angle to cast-off sts at armhole on back and front.

Shallow set-in sleeves: Place centre of cast off edge of sleeve to shoulder seam. Match decreases at beg of armhole shaping to decreases at top of sleeve. Sew sleeve head into armhole, easing in shapings.

Set-in sleeves: Place centre of cast-off edge of sleeve to shoulder seam. Set in sleeve, easing sleeve head into armhole. Join side and sleeve seams.
Slip stitch pocket edgings and linings into place.
Sew on buttons to correspond with buttonholes.
Ribbed welts and neckbands and any areas of garter stitch should not be pressed.

ABBREVIATIONS

K	knit
P	purl
st(s)	stitch(es)
inc	increas(e)(ing)
dec	decreas(e)(ing)
st st	stocking stitch (1 row K, 1 row P)
g st	garter stitch (K every row)
beg	begin(ning)
foll	following
rem	remain(ing)
rev st st	reverse stocking stitch (1 row K , 1 row P)
rep	repeat
alt	alternate
cont	continue
patt	pattern
tog	together
mm	millimetres
cm	centimetres
in(s)	inch(es)
RS	right side
WS	wrong side
sl 1	slip one stitch
psso	pass slipped stitch over
p2sso	pass 2 slipped stitches over
tbl	through back of loop
M1	make one stitch by picking up horizontal loop before next stitch and knitting into back of it
M1P	make one stitch by picking up horizontal loop before next stitch and purlinginto back of it
yfwd	yarn forward
yrn	yarn round needle
meas	measures
0	no stitches, times or rows
-	no stitches, times or rows for that size
yo	yarn over needle
yfrn	yarn forward round needle
wyib	with yarn at back
sl2togK	slip 2 stitches together knitways

MACHINE WASH SYMBOLS

HAND WASH SYMBOLS

DRY CLEAN SYMBOLS

IRONING SYMBOLS

DO NOT BLEACH SYMBOL

DRYING SYMBOLS